# Things People with Disabilities Are Allowed to Do
## (An Incomplete List)

Elizabeth Pickett

Things People with Disabilities Are Allowed to Do
(An Incomplete List)

Paperback Edition: 979-8-9939525-0-5

Copyright © 2025 Elizabeth Pickett
All rights reserved.

No part of this publication may be reproduced, stored, or transmitted
in any form or by any means without the prior written permission of the author,
except in the case of brief quotations used in reviews or scholarly work.

People with disabilities are allowed to be asked their opinion

People with disabilities are allowed to be leaders

People with disabilities are allowed to make their own decisions

People with disabilities are allowed to dance

People with disabilities are allowed to be heard

People with disabilities are allowed to be in the community

People with disabilities are allowed to voice their thoughts

People with disabilities are allowed to eat in public

People with disabilities are allowed to love others

People with disabilities are allowed to be in meaningful relationships

People with disabilities are allowed to make financial decisions

People with disabilities are allowed access to concerts and public places

People with disabilities are allowed to decide who they want to talk to about their situations

People with disabilities are allowed to go to the mall

People with disabilities are allowed to do art

People with disabilities are allowed to have access to sidewalks

People with disabilities are allowed to drive

People with disabilities are allowed to have good healthcare

People with disabilities are allowed to live in a caring environment outside of institutions

People with disabilities are allowed to have respect and dignity

People with disabilities are allowed to look good

People with disabilities are allowed to have families

People with disabilities are allowed to travel

People with disabilities are allowed to pursue education

People with disabilities are allowed to work in any field

People with disabilities are allowed to own businesses

People with disabilities are allowed to be creative

People with disabilities are allowed to enjoy sports and recreation

People with disabilities are allowed to rest without guilt

People with disabilities are allowed to vote and participate in politics

People with disabilities are allowed to dream big

People with disabilities are allowed to be loved

People with disabilities are allowed to be parents

People with disabilities are allowed to live independently

36

People with disabilities are allowed to seek adventure

People with disabilities are allowed to be proud of themselves

People with disabilities have the right to live fully, love deeply, dream boldly, and pursue joy—just like everyone else. Their rights, choices, and dignity are not special privileges, but reflections of the same intrinsic worth that every human being possesses.

# Overcoming Ableism

Overcoming ableism requires awareness, empathy, and a commitment to valuing all people equally — not for their abilities, but for their humanity. Here are some important lessons and actions that can help individuals and communities challenge bias and promote true inclusion:

## 1. Education and Awareness

Learning About Disability: Understand that disability is part of human diversity, not something to be fixed or pitied.

Language Matters: Use respectful, person-first or identity-first language according to individual preference.

## 2. Listening and Respect

Center Lived Experience: Listen to people with disabilities instead of speaking for them.

Respect Autonomy: Avoid making decisions on someone's behalf without their input or consent.

## 3. Dignity and Equality

Value All Lives Equally: Recognize that disabled lives are complete and meaningful — not "broken" or "less than."

Reject Pity and Inspiration Tropes: Don't frame people with disabilities as objects of pity or as "inspirational" for simply living their lives.

## 4. Faith and Sensitivity

Reconsider "Healing" Narratives: Praying for someone's disability to be removed can imply that they are incomplete. Instead, pray for accessibility, justice, and understanding.

Honor Wholeness: See each person as already whole and valuable, exactly as they are. leadership roles.

## 5. Accessibility and Inclusion

Physical Access: Support accessible environments — ramps, captions, interpreters, and inclusive design.

Social Access: Include people with disabilities in community life, friendships, workplaces, and leadership roles.

## 6. Allyship and Advocacy

Speak Up: Challenge ableist jokes, stereotypes, or systems when you encounter them.

Amplify Voices: Share the work, writing, and leadership of disabled advocates and creators.

## 7. Representation and Visibility

Inclusive Media: Support authentic representation of people with disabilities in media, education, and art.

Normalize Diversity: Help children see disability as a natural part of the human experience.

## 8. Empathy and Connection

See the Person, Not the Diagnosis: Remember that every person has dreams, talents, and value beyond their disability.

Build Relationships: Approach others with curiosity, compassion, and equality — not charity or pity.

## 9. Responsibility and Growth

Acknowledge Bias: Recognize your own assumptions and work to unlearn them.
Keep Learning: Disability inclusion is an ongoing process — stay open to correction and growth.

## 10. Building an Inclusive Future

Community Change: Support policies and practices that ensure full participation for everyone.

Celebrate Diversity: Embrace a world where every person — disabled or not — belongs, contributes, and thrives.

*By fostering understanding, access, and genuine respect, we move closer to a society where disability is not seen as a limitation, but as a natural and valuable part of human life.*

Inclusivity starts with you.
Be the change we need in the world.

www.ingramcontent.com/pod-product-compliance
Lightning Source LLC
Chambersburg PA
CBHW042359030426
42337CB00032B/5159